# The Armor of God

### By Phillip Rich

**EKKLISIA PROPHETIC
APOSTOLIC MINISTRIES, INC.**

Copyright © 2012 by Phillip Rich

*The Armor of God*
by Phillip Rich

Printed in the United States of America

ISBN 9781619964006

All rights reserved solely by the author. The author guarantees all contents are original and do not infringe upon the legal rights of any other person or work. No part of this publication may be reproduced, stored in a retrieval system, or transmitted, in whole or in part, in any form or by any means, electronic, mechanical, photocopying, recording or otherwise, without the prior express consent of the author. The views expressed in this book are not necessarily those of the publisher.

Unless otherwise indicated, Bible quotations are taken from The King James Version. Brackets reflect the author's added emphasis.

Take note that the name satan is not capitalized. The author chooses not to acknowledge him, even to the point of violating grammatical rules.

www.xulonpress.com

# *Table of Contents*

*Introduction* ............................................................... *9*

*The Belt of Truth* ..................................................... *11*

*Breastplate of Righteousness* ............................................ *21*

*Shoes of the Gospel of Peace* ........................................... *31*

*The Shield of Faith* ................................................... *42*

*Helmet of Salvation* ................................................... *53*

*Sword of the Spirit* ................................................... *65*

*Conclusion* ............................................................. *73*

# SPECIAL THANKS

About the Editor: Greg Pettys and his wife, Johnita, have been a big support and encouragement to me and my ministry. They have a lovely family and live in Springfield, Ill. Greg works as a financial consultant and is also an anointed author and prophetic teacher. Greg has spent much time spearheading the publishing of this book without whose prayers, encouragement and financial support this book may have never been published.

Also, I want to thank our office staff, Ryan and Rachel Shannon and Dolores Duncan for their time spent making corrections, proofing and rewriting what was needed. Also, a special thanks to my wife, Connie Rich, for her love and support and assistance in finalizing the completion of this book.

I want to give the utmost thanks to the Holy Spirit for releasing this revelation at such an opportune time to the body of Christ.

# FORWARD

When the Lord assigned me the privilege of partnering with Apostle Prophet Phil Rich to get this book published I set aside a day to dive into his rough draft. Three months later I was still getting fresh revelation from the Lord on the Armor of God.

Though most of us know something about the Armor of God or even have heard or preached good sermons on the topic, what I have found is a truly new dimension of understanding from being immersed in this project.

There is a very powerful and practical depth of revelation in these pages springing from the Word of God out of the life of a man that has used this Armor of God in some dangerous and very challenging places all over the world the last 40 years!

Each dynamic piece of God's Armor as described in his book has been tested much in Phil's mission outreaches to such places as Nepal, Bhutan, Bangladesh, Cambodia, Vietnam, Singapore, Peru, Germany, Israel, Russia, and Tajikistan with more countries to come. When his very life was in danger God's Armor has sheltered him. When health and finances were contested God came through by using the Armor of God as found in this book.

As you progress through each chapter with the expectation to receive from God you will find faith building from the Lord will occur. Plus what happened with me is that you will be able to use these Armor pieces to enter new ground, new territories, and take new places toward fulfilling your Divine Destiny.

Even those who have worn the Armor of God well all their Christian lives will find ways to tighten that belt of Truth and enlarge the shield of faith. You will have strength to stand and having done all to stand victoriously in your life's purpose, health, finances, marriage, and ministry!

Once you start reading you will not want to put this book down! Get ready to put on the complete and customized Armor of God more effectively than ever before. Let's go slay some giants together!

Greg S. Pettys

# INTRODUCTION

The Word of God is a shield and a buckler. It will heal me if I know how to plant it in my heart. The Word of God will prosper me if I will place it deep in my heart and walk in it. The Word of God will even speak to me and reveal to me by the Spirit the way I should go.

I am going to share some thoughts that will enable us to walk in victory. They will enable us to not only be on the defensive against satan, but to also be on the offensive. We will have not only a great defensive line, but a fantastic offensive line and we are going to beat the devil into the ground. We are not going to stand for him defeating us anymore.

The church has taken one too many beatings, has been in the muck and the mire, down on Grumble Street next to Grumble Alley defeated, pressed down and stepped on. I am sick and tired of being sick and tired. I am upset with the devil. As far as I am concerned satan has had his day, but he hasn't had his way. Jesus is still Lord, still the one I adore. We are going to walk on the devil, tread on our trouble. He is under our feet and not over our head. We are the ones who are supposed to bruise his head with our heel. We are the ones to walk in victory over satan defeating the enemy and nothing shall hurt us.

**Ephesians 6:10-11; "Finally** [getting to the end of the matter], **my brethren, be strong in the Lord, and in the power of his might. Put on the whole armour of God, that ye may be able to stand against the wiles of the devil."**

Stand does not mean that you are just standing and letting the devil repeatedly beat you in the face. It means to stand up against him, to start slugging it out with him. It doesn't mean that you are just going to let him take shots at you. It is time to stand up against the devil and tell him "No more. It is over. You have had your day and now it's time for Jesus to have His day in my life."

**Ephesians 6:12-13; "For we wrestle not against flesh and blood, but against principalities, against powers, against the rulers of the darkness of this world, against spiritual wickedness in high places. Wherefore take unto you the whole armor of God, that ye may be able to withstand in the evil day, and having done all, to stand."**

Withstand means to stand against and fight. It doesn't mean that you are just holding the fort, waving a little flag of truce, hoping that somehow you can just hang on to the end. God doesn't want you to just hang on to the end. You are not to be a defeated person and God doesn't want you to be defeated. He wants you to overcome through the blood of Jesus. That is the reason Jesus died on the cross. He spoiled principalities, and powers, made a show of them openly. He triumphed over them so that you and I could also triumph over them in it.[1]

# THE BELT OF TRUTH

**Ephesians 6:14; "Stand therefore, having your loins girt about with truth, and having on the breastplate of righteousness;'**

Your loins are the part of you that will produce the Word of God. The procreative part of you spiritually is just like it is the procreative part of you physically. If you totally surround yourself with that which is truth, that which is reality from the Word of God, then you are girding your loins about with truth and you will start producing that truth in your life. That is why Jesus could tell us in John 8:31-32, "If you continue in my word, then are ye my disciples indeed; and ye shall know the truth, and the truth shall make you free."

The truth is not only something that is protective. It is also something that becomes an offensive weapon against the devil. The best way to come against error is to show people the truth. The best way to come against and fight error is with the truth. With that which is reality, with that which is genuine you are able to fight that which is in error. You fight it with reality.

The first time T.L. Osborn had a chance to go to India as a missionary, he tried to share the facts of the Word, not the acts, with the people. He went to talk to the nationals and to share with them about Jesus Christ. They believed Jesus Christ lived upon the earth, that He was a great man of God, that He was a prophet of God. But they did not believe He was the Son of God. He tried his best to share the truth with them, but they would not receive it. He came back to

America discouraged, ready to quit his ministry as a missionary because he had no converts in India.

He went to a meeting where Brother William Branham was preaching. Brother Branham was mightily used by God in tent meetings and in meetings in large coliseums. Deaf and crippled people were brought into his meetings. Those people would be healed and set free right in front of the eyes of the crowd. The deaf would always hear. The blind would always see. Anyone who needed healing would be healed in his ministry.

Brother Osborn sat there watching God do the mighty works of the Word. God spoke to him and said, "If you will take that to India, you will win India for me." So he took it back to India. He had crowds of two to three hundred thousand. Thousands gave their heart to God as they saw the truth. If truth is truth, it can be manifested. God is not afraid to prove Himself to hungry hearts.

He doesn't want to prove Himself to religious folks who don't care to know, don't want to know anyway and are trying to make a laughing stock out of it. He will not give signs and wonders to a perverse generation that does not care. Jesus was referring to religious people, the Scribes and the Pharisees who wanted Him to show them a sign. They didn't care about a sign. They just wanted to make a mockery out of Him.

He will manifest Himself to people who really want to know the truth, are hungry for the truth, are looking for the truth, desire to find the truth, the reality, that which is genuine and that which can be proven from God's holy Word. It is high time that we get hold of the Word and dig in until we find from the Word what really works in our lives.

Ever heard of practical theology? If we have all this knowledge and are not doing any of it, it isn't very practical is it? You can gain a knowledge of God and never know Him. You can gain a knowledge of God and never know His ways, never know what He is really like, never really know

Him as a person and know Him in the power of His resurrection. God wants us to know truth. Jesus said in John 14:6, "I am the way. I am the truth. I am the light. No man cometh to the Father but by Me." He began to share that He is what is real and what is genuine. That is part of us if we know how to surround our loins with the truth of the Word of God, with the Word of God that will produce, with the Word of God that is real. That part which can be proven by the Spirit of God and can be shown forth in your life by the Spirit of God will gird about your loins as a protective covering as well as being a weapon against error.

Surround yourself with truth. If you have experienced salvation in your life and have experienced Jesus Christ as your Lord, that is truth to you. If you have experienced healing in your life, you have experienced truth. If you have experienced the provision of God in your life, [2] that is truth to you. To another person, it may not be truth because they may not have yet experienced the manifestation of the Word of God in their life.

God wants us to have practical theology. He wants us to walk in the Word, wants the Word to work in our lives. He wants us to work the Word of God, to find that which it truth and walk in it, manifest it. Don't just tell somebody how they ought to live, show them how to live. That is truth. Don't just tell somebody about healing. Show them they can be healed by the Word of God. Lay hands on them and manifest healing in their bodies. That is truth.

**Acts 1:8; "But ye shall receive power, after that the Holy Ghost is come upon you: and ye shall be witnesses unto me both in Jerusalem, and in all Judaea, and in Samaria, and unto the uttermost part of the earth."**

Did you know the disciples, many of whom where later called the twelve apostles, were told to do something in Acts1:8? We have not understood that. We thought Acts 1:8

meant we are to go and verbally witness to people. That is not what it is saying. Jesus didn't say to just go and tell others about Him. Most of those people had heard about Jesus. They would say, "Big deal" just like the people in India did.

Study every verse in the book of Acts where it talks about them bearing witness. How did they do it? With signs, wonders and diverse miracles and gifts of the Holy Ghost they bore witness of the truth. So how do I share truth? Not just with facts, but with acts. If I believe in healing, I am going to show healing. If I believe someone needs to be born again, I will show them how to be born again and help them get that way. That is the truth. If I believe in deliverance and see someone who is bound up, I am going to tell them about it and help them get free. That is truth. It is not enough just to tell people. It is time to show people.

I had a chance to go a meeting where a man of God was teaching how to lay hands on the sick and minister healing. He was teaching in a seminar on the Holy Ghost. He said he had healing teams in his church that would go out to help people. After the people got healed, they would get saved. That is how they witnessed.

A couple of ladies, who were members of his church, walked up to some men who had just gotten off an airplane and asked them if they believed in God, in Jesus, and that God could do wondrous miracles and things. They answered that they didn't believe in Jesus. They worshipped someone else. They didn't believe Jesus was real. The women asked if they could lay hands on them and prove that Jesus is real would they then accept Jesus. The men answered yes, if they could prove it. These ladies laid hands on those two gentlemen and started praying. The men started shaking from head to toe. They shook so much that they started weeping, fell to their knees and began crying out for Jesus.

What is truth?

Another man I know spent a lot of time praying and seeking the Lord. Some Jehovah Witnesses came to his door wanting to meet with him. They said they were bible students and just wanted to ask some questions. While they were trying to sell books, give him the Watchtower and talk about other things he sat there and asked God to tell him how to reach them. The Lord told him to reach over and slap one of them in the face. He told the Lord he couldn't do that. God said that if he would, then He would manifest His glory and He would reach the men. He obeyed God, reached over and slapped one on the side of the cheek. It was like a chain reaction and all of them were knocked off the couch onto the floor. They were all grabbing their mouths. They all had cavities in their teeth and God had completely filled them. They all got saved that day.

That is truth. If Jesus really is alive He will manifest Himself if you believe it. The reason He doesn't more often is because people don't believe it. Either we have a reality or we have something that it fictional. Either we really serve the Lord and we believe it or we are playing games. My Jesus is alive, and I believe what I am talking about. I know my Lord. I talked to Him today. He is very real and very concerned about you. Jesus wants to move in your life and manifest truth to you. When He manifests His truth to you it will set you free and you will be able to gird about your loins with it.

If you ever fight illness and get a hold of the truth of healing, you will be able to master it. You will gird about your loins in a way that satan will never be able to come against you with illness like he did before. Once you master the truth of that and gird about your loins with it you can walk in healing. You can walk in the manifestation of healing in your life with the Lord manifesting His healing power to you all the time on a consistent basis.

He is not Jehovah Rapha for just those certain little instances when you need it. He is Jehovah Rapha all the time. He is Jehovah Rapha when you get up in the morning. He is Jehovah Rapha when you go to bed at night. He is Jehovah Rapha when you brush your teeth and look at yourself in the mirror. He is Jehovah Rapha when you sit down at the breakfast table to eat. He is Jehovah Rapha when you sit down at lunch. He is Jehovah Rapha when you eat your evening meal. He is there twenty-four hours a day to manifest His healing power and His glory to you. The truth is that He is the Lord God that healeth thee. That is the truth and that truth will set you free from sickness. This is different from what we have been told before.

What about finances? We need to get hold of the fact that my God shall supply all my need according to His riches in glory by Christ Jesus and not just at certain times. He wants to be your supply officer. He wants to be there to supply what you have need of all the time. He is Jehovah Jireh in the middle of the night. He is Jehovah Jireh when there are bills coming in. He is Jehovah Jireh when there are no bills coming in. He is Jehovah Jirah when you have money in your pocket. He is Jehovah Jireh when you don't have a dime in your pocket. He is Jehovah Jireh all the time. He said, "I am the Lord God. I change not." He stays the same. In James it says that in Him there isn't even a little shadow of turning.[3] He will always be Jehovah Jireh your provider, the One who meets all of your needs according to His riches in glory by Christ Jesus.

God will do it in the morning if you will yield to it. He will do it at night if you will yield to it. He will do it all day long if you will yield to it. The Lord is just waiting for you to get a hold of it, for you to gird about your loins with the truth that He is Jehovah Jirah. Then surround yourself with the facts, surround yourself with the acts, surround yourself with the manifestation of Jehovah Jirah all day long.

He is Jehovah Jireh all the time and not a part time God. He is my full time God and I am His full time child. I am concerned about my children all the time. If they have a need I am thinking about it even when they are sleeping. Don't you think the heavenly Father is the same way? He is thinking about us. The one thing that causes Him to activate His character towards you is your faith in Him. When you begin to trust Him to be Jehovah Jireh, you look up in His face and say, "Oh, Father, you are Jehovah Jireh to me. You are my provider. You are the one who meets my every need and I worship and praise you for being Jehovah Jireh." When you claim Him as Jehovah Jireh, He will be Jehovah Jireh to you. He will be your provider.

You have to claim Him by faith. You have to surround yourself with that truth. Totally surround yourself with truth and get permeated with it. Get infiltrated with it. Get wrapped up in it. Get full of the truth that He is Jehovah Jirah, your provider and His grace is more than sufficient for you.

He is also El Shaddai, more than enough to meet your every need. He is more than enough to take care of your family. He is more than enough to take care of you in every way, shape or form, physically, financially or otherwise. He is concerned about you. That is the truth.

When you know the truth, the truth will make you free. It didn't just say that if you know some facts the truth will make you free. It says to know that which is real, that which is genuine. Understand the character of God. Too many times we try to study the Bible and we don't understand the One who wrote it. I don't care what anybody thinks the scriptures say, what does God say? He wrote it. Be students of the Word and sit before the Holy Spirit asking Him to reveal to us the truth because it the truth that will set us free and not a set of facts that we look up in our concordance.

"Help me to know the character of God. Spirit of the living God, reveal to me the whole counsel of God. Reveal to me the plan of God. Reveal to me what I can have in Jesus Christ for my life."

## SPIRIT OF TRUTH

The Holy Ghost is called the spirit of truth.

**John 16:13-15; "Howbeit when He, the Spirit of truth, is come, He will guide you into all truth: for He shall not speak of himself; but whatsoever He shall hear, that shall He speak: and He will show you things to come. He shall glorify me: for He shall receive of mine, and shall show it unto you. All things that the Father hath are mine: therefore said I, that He shall take of mine, and shall show it unto you."**

The Holy Spirit will guide you into what is real and what is genuine. The Spirit of God will show you things. When the Holy Ghost starts revealing the truth to you, starts showing you what is truth, you can walk in it and it will manifest. When you begin to ask the Holy Spirit to show you truths from the Word, He will not show you something that is off the wall and not in the Word. The Spirit and the Word are in agreement.[3] They will not contradict one another; you can stand on the Word of God and know that the Word and the Spirit are in agreement.

When the Holy Spirit begins to show you the Word, He will lead you to the Word. As He leads you to the Word, He will begin to reveal the Word. As He reveals the Word the light comes on in your life. Darkness begins to dispel and then you begin to see how you can do that Word.

The very next thing the Holy Spirit will lead you into is the action of that truth. The Holy Spirit will never reveal anything to you for you to just to bear the truth and hold it to yourself. He will reveal something to you so that you can act on it, so that you can share it. He will lead you to act on it.

Join hands with the Holy Ghost and ask the Spirit of God to manifest the fruit of that truth in your life. Begin to yield yourself to what the Holy Spirit is saying. He will not guide you amiss, but will guide you into all truth. He will guide you into truth, not away from it. When you come to the truth, the truth will be able to make you free when you act on it.

We need the manifestation of salvation to come through our lives. Salvation is an all-inclusive term. In the Greek, salvation is soteria. It means salvation that is given to you by God. You receive it by faith and it covers every part of your being spirit, soul and body. When He came to save you from sin, He also came to save you from sickness, from poverty and from the bondage of the devil. Salvation means being saved from sin, being healed, prospered, set free, made everywhere whole by the power of God. Romans 10:9-10 tells us how to get salvation. We know it is all-inclusive, so how do we get it?

**Romans 10:9-10 "That if thou shalt confess with thy mouth the Lord Jesus** [Lordship over my finances, Lordship over my spirit, Lordship over my body, Lordship over my family], **and shalt believe in thine heart** [that is how man believes the things that are right] **that God hath raised him from the dead, thou shalt be saved. For with the heart man believeth unto righteousness; and with the mouth confession is made unto** [full and complete] **salvation."**

We are healed the same way we are saved from sin. It is by saying, "Jesus, you are Lord over my physical body. In Jesus' name I am healed. I believe in my heart Jesus rose again on the third day. I believe by the power of the Holy Ghost that the same Spirit that raised Christ from the dead dwells in me. This same Spirit that raised Christ from the dead now is inside of me, quickening my mortal body by the Spirit of the Lord."

Romans 8:11 tells us that the Spirit who raised up Jesus from the dead is the same Spirit who heals your body. He raises you up physically the same way He raised Jesus up from the grave. Romans 8:11 is not talking about the great resurrection. It is talking about our physical bodies. It is talking about healing.

When you let the truth dawn on you, it is like all the light bulbs in town being in one place and turned on at the same time. All the darkness is dispelled and you start saying, "Yes, that is my Jesus. That's my Lord. That is how He really is. He is my Healer. He is my Provider the same way He saves me from sin. He heals my body and that is the same way He meets my needs because He is concerned about me. Father, I believe, and I confess that you meet all my needs according to your riches in glory by Christ Jesus. I praise you for it. I thank you for being my Provider."

# BREASTPLATE OF RIGHTEOUSNESS

We are still looking at the armor and how to use it. The armor is different from the weapons although the armor is also armament. It can be used in a weapon-like fashion.

**Ephesians 6:10-14; "Finally, my brethren, be strong in the Lord, and in the power of his might. Put on the whole armour of God, that ye may be able to stand against the wiles of the devil. For we wrestle not against flesh and blood, but against principalities, against powers, against the rulers of the darkness of this world, against spiritual wickedness in high places. Wherefore take unto you the whole armour of God, that ye may be able to withstand in the evil day, and having done all, to stand. Stand therefore, having your loins girt about with truth, and having on the breastplate of righteousness;"**

What is the breastplate of righteousness? How do we put it on?

We can look at the armor and say yes the Bible says that we are to put on the armor, be totally covered with the armor of God because we are in a battle. But how do we put this armor on? It is a little different from the armor you would put on if you were going into natural combat against an enemy force. So, how do we put God's armor on? What does each part of that armor represent to me as a Christian? We will find out that it is not only defensive, but also offensive. It works in a way that enables you to come against satan effectively. It becomes a weapon against the devil.

The Greek word for breastplate is thorax. It means the covering, that which covers the front part of you, your vital organs, the heart, the part of you that keeps you alive. The breastplate is a covering of righteousness. Righteousness means to be able to stand in the presence of God without fear, without guilt, without a feeling of inferiority. In Genesis 3 we see that three things took place when man sinned and lost righteousness.

**Genesis 3:8-10; "And they heard the voice of the LORD God walking in the garden in the cool of the day: and Adam and his wife hid themselves from the presence of the LORD God amongst the trees of the garden. And the LORD God called unto Adam, and said unto him, Where art thou? And he said, I heard thy voice in the garden, and I was afraid, because I was naked; and I hid myself."**

Adam and Eve had lost their covering, their thorax. Now they noticed that they were naked. Some may say they were naked before, but they never realized it. No, they were clothed in the righteousness of God. They had a covering and it was a right relationship with God. They never were afraid before.

Fear was one of the things that happened to Adam and Eve when they lost their clothing of righteousness. Unrighteousness brings about fear. Fear of God, fear of the devil, fear of circumstances, fear of everything. You are totally afraid something is going to happen to you, that is not going to be good and you actually believe it will happen. That is one of the byproducts of unrighteousness.

Another thing that happened was they tried to find their own clothing. They put fig leaves together to cover themselves, went to find their own righteousness. God tells us that our righteousness is as filthy rags in His sight. It will never do. It will never hold up. God had to come and give them a different type of clothing. Our righteousness will never be what it ought to be. That covering is inferior and it will not replace God's righteousness. So, Adam and Eve were afraid and put on their own type of righteousness.

Something else they did was to hide. They were no longer in the place with God that they were before. They were no longer in right standing with God. They no longer walked with God in the cool of the evening to commune with Him. How could they? They were hiding in the trees. They didn't run out and say, "Hello, God. It is wonderful to see you. Let's walk together." No, they couldn't because they were hiding.

When you and I lose the righteousness of God in Christ Jesus because of sin and because of broken relationship then we are not able to walk with God the way we should walk with Him.

Jesus came to restore righteousness to mankind, to give us that righteousness again so that we could walk in right standing with God without fear, without guilt, without inferiority, without believing that the worst is going to take place. We can have a relationship with God where we can walk boldly into the throne room of God and make our petitions known unto Him. We can do that without fear, without inferiority, without feeling like there is no way that we can approach God. It is true that you can't approach God in your own righteousness. You can't go before God with your own merit. You and I have none. We don't have to go with our own righteousness because Jesus came and paid a price to restore and to give back to mankind the righteousness of God in Christ Jesus. That righteousness of God in Christ Jesus is what we are going to talk about.

**Ephesians 2:13-16 "But now in Christ Jesus ye who sometimes were far off are made nigh by the blood of Christ. For he is our peace, who hath made both one, and hath broken down the middle wall of partition between us; Having abolished in his flesh the enmity, even the law**

of commandments contained in ordinances; for to make in himself of twain one new man, so making peace; and that He might reconcile both unto God in one body by the cross, having slain the enmity thereby.

Sin came up as a mighty wall between God and man. The blood of Jesus has slain the enmity, slain the sin, slain that which came between God and man.

**Ephesians 2:17-19; "And came and preached peace to you which were afar off, and to them that were nigh. For through him we both have access by one Spirit unto the Father. Now therefore ye are no more strangers and foreigners, but fellow citizens with the saints, and of the household of God;"**

We become something that we weren't before. Before we were strangers, foreigners, now we become part of the household of faith. Before we were not family, now we are children of God, part of the bloodline. His blood flows through my veins. That is why I don't walk with fear, inferiority and guilt complexes. I am not the man I used to be. If any man be in Christ, he is a brand new creature. Old things have passed away and behold all things become new.[5] I am a new creation now and part of the family, part of His family. I am flesh of His flesh, bone of His bone. He has given this to me.

**Romans 5:17; "For if by one man's offence death reigned by one; much more they which receive abundance of grace and of the gift of righteousness shall reign in life by one, Jesus Christ.)"**

By grace and this gift of righteousness I shall reign in this life because I am not the man I used to be. I am a new creation in Christ Jesus. I have been made to overcome. Jesus

Christ has made me to rule in this life. This life is not to rule and reign over me because I have a place of authority through Jesus. I have a place of rulership through the Lord and now rule and reign over my problem. Now satan is under my feet. Whatever I have need of, I can just speak the Word and command it to take place. I am in a place of authority. No longer the tail, I am now the head. No longer a worm in the dust, I am a king's kid, an heir of God, a joint heir with Jesus Christ.

**2 Corinthians 5:21; "For he hath made him to be sin for us, who knew no sin; that we might be made the righteousness of God in him."**

Jesus took our place so that we might be made the righteousness of God in Him. It is a gift. We are made righteous. It is not something that we can do. We have to accept it. Romans 3:22 tell us how we can receive this place of authority, this place of sonship rights and abilities.

**Romans 3:22; "Even the righteousness of God which is by faith of Jesus Christ unto all and upon all them that believe: for there is no difference:"**

We have to receive it by faith. If we believe in Jesus, accept what He did on the cross, accept that He abolished the enmity between us and God, accept that He has come to strip me of all unrighteousness and to place on us the stamp of righteousness then it becomes ours in Jesus' Name.

But what if I fail? What if I do wrong?

**1 John 1:9; "If we confess our sins, he is faithful and just to forgive us our sins, and to cleanse us from all unrighteousness."**

If you have just been cleansed from all unrighteousness, all the unrighteousness is gone and you become righteous in His sight with His righteousness that He has given you as a child of God. It is a gift. You have been made righteous. You have been made in right standing with God. By ourselves we are never worthy. He has given us His righteousness and has covered us with His blood. When the Father looks at us He doesn't see unworthiness, doesn't see unrighteousness. He sees the blood of His Son, the blood of the Lamb. He sees the righteousness of God in Christ Jesus.

Does that mean I can live the way I want to live? It means that I can remain in a place of righteousness if I so chose to. If I sin and confess my sin, all unrighteousness will be wiped out of my life. We are supposed to live in this righteousness. It is not something we put on one time and we are ever careful to retain. Once God gives you something you have to keep it. You have to keep your healing. Sometimes the devil tries to steal from you. If he can take it from you, he will try. But you don't have to give in to him.

**1 Peter 2:24; "Who his own self bare our sins in his own body on the tree, that we, being dead to sins, should live unto righteousness: by whose stripes ye were healed."**

We are to live in this right standing with God. We are to live in this place of authority with God.

**Ephesians 1:20-23; "Which he wrought in Christ, when he raised him from the dead, and set him at his own right hand in the heavenly places, Far above all principality, and power, and might, and dominion, and every name that is named, not only in this world, but also in that which is to come: And hath put all things under his feet, and gave him to be the head over all things to the church, Which is his body, the fulness of him that filleth all in all."**

We have been placed in heavenly places with Christ Jesus. Satan is under our feet. Demon powers are under our feet. Sickness and disease are under our feet. Guilt, inferiority, or fear is under our feet. If fear tries to rise up against you, get it under your feet. If sickness tries to come up against you, get it under your feet. If satan tries to bring back to you things you once did, tell him that man is dead. That man is gone. Those things are under the blood. Old things are passed away and all things have become new. God doesn't remember it and I can chose to forget it. I am not going to allow satan's remembrance to hinder my faith. What I once was is under the blood, under His righteousness. It is totally covered, wiped out, washed away by His blood. His blood washes away every stain. Any remembrance of it satan has. He is the accuser of the brethren. If satan can bring condemnation and guilt against us, our faith will begin to waver. Our authority will begin to waver. Our righteousness will begin to waver.

That is why we have to stand up by faith and live in righteousness. It becomes a mighty sword and weapon against the devil. If you know you are in right standing with God, then look out satan and demons. You are not going to mess around with them. You are not going to put up with them. You are not going to put up with sickness or disease. You won't put up with poverty and lack. You won't put up with sin because you will rise up in a place of authority and righteousness in Jesus Christ. You will put satan under your feet and keep him there. That is when you walk in His righteousness, when you live in His righteousness. Not your own.

Remember satan is going to bring memories of the past. He will bring memories of your failures, but you don't have to accept his remembrance. You accept the remembrance of God when He says He separates those things as far as the east is from the west in the sea of His forgetfulness, never to be remembered anymore. That is the only remembrance you are going to accept. If God forgets it, you are going to do your best to forget it. You are not going to go by satan's remembrance. You are not going to let him do that to you. You are going to tell him off and put him back under your feet.

God wants us to live in righteousness and dwell in righteousness. He wants us to rise up in righteousness day by day with the righteousness He has given us. With righteousness we overcome the unrighteousness that satan would like to try and bring against us. We overcome sin with righteousness. We overcome the lusts of our flesh with the righteousness of God.

**Romans 6:12-13; "Let not sin therefore reign in your mortal body, that ye should obey it in the lusts thereof. Neither yield ye your members as instruments of unrighteousness unto sin: but yield yourselves unto God, as those that are alive from the dead, and your members as instruments of righteousness unto God."**

You make a choice to live in righteousness. You make a choice to overcome by the righteousness of God that is in you. You make a choice for sin not to have dominion over you. You have dominion over it. It is under your feet.

**Romans 6:14-17; "For sin shall not have dominion over you: for ye are not under the law, but under grace. What then? shall we sin, because we are not under the law, but under grace? God forbid. Know ye not, that to whom ye yield yourselves servants to obey, his servants ye are to whom ye obey; whether of sin unto death, or of obedience unto righteousness? But God be thanked, that ye were the servants of sin, but ye have obeyed from the heart that form of doctrine which was delivered you."**

What form of doctrine is that? The doctrine of righteousness. The righteousness of God makes you free from the law of sin and death. It frees us from the bondages and dominion of sin. Now you must let the righteousness of God flourish within you. You must live in that righteousness and see yourself not as a worm in the dust, but as a child of God, an heir of God, a joint heir of Jesus Christ, an overcomer in this life. See yourself that way. Walk in that and you will be able to overcome sin.

You can overcome sin with the righteousness of God in Christ. Sin will not be able to rule over you when you stand up and say, "I am somebody in Jesus. I am an heir of God. I am a joint heir with Jesus Christ. I have been made the righteousness of God in Christ Jesus. I am not the man I used to be. I am a brand new creation, a brand new man. I walk in a place of authority with God, in a place of relationship with God. I will walk in power on this earth and I will not walk in defeat. I will not allow satan to come against my mind with thoughts of inferiority, with thoughts of nothingness, with thoughts that I am a nobody. I will not allow satan to put those thoughts in my mind. I will put them under my feet and I will walk in a place of authority with God."

Satan is under your feet. When you learn this you will control your mind and what thoughts come in. That is how satan will try to dominate you. He'll say, "You remember what you did? You remember how you always fail? You remember you have never been a success before?"

You can say, "Satan shut up. That man is dead. I have the authority of God. I have the righteousness of God in Christ Jesus inside of me. I can run through a troop and leap over a wall. I can do all things through Christ Jesus who give me the strength. I will succeed with His success. I will overcome with His overcoming power, I am everything through Jesus.

I am nothing by myself, but I am not by myself. God won't leave you alone to fail. If you tie in with Him and join hands with Him you will succeed. Someway, somehow you are going to make it. I can't always tell you how, but I know you will if you will join hands with His righteousness. Come into right relationship with God.

It will change your prayer life. If you come into right relationship with God, you will come into prayer and be able to say, "Father, in the Name of Jesus, I thank you that today I have power and authority over all devils. I thank you that I can walk over the devil and he is under my feet. I can do all things through Christ Jesus who strengthens me. Therefore, satan, turn loose of the finances that are mine. Let go of my physical body in Jesus' Name. I am in covenant with the Word and the testimony, with the blood of the Lamb. I overcome in Jesus' Name." That is how you will start praying. That is how you start acting. Those demons of sickness will be afraid of you. Those discouraging devils will start hiding when you come along because they don't want to get beat up again. You tore them up the last time and they couldn't take it.

You can walk in a place of authority in God. You can live in His righteousness. It is yours.

# SHOES OF THE GOSPEL OF PEACE

**Ephesians 6:13-15; "Wherefore take unto you the whole armour of God, that ye may be able to withstand in the evil day, and having done all, to stand. Stand therefore, having your loins girt about with truth, and having on the breastplate of righteousness; And your feet shod with the preparation of the gospel of peace;"**

Stand does not mean you are trying to hold back the forces of darkness. It means you are standing up against, offensively attacking the forces of darkness. It is not "I can't quite hold them off. Lord, you are going to have to send some reinforcements." It is not like that at all.

I am advancing with the shield of faith. I am advancing with the sword of the Spirit. I am moving forward against the gates of hell and they will not prevail against me. I am moving against, standing against, withstanding satan. I am not moving backwards, barely holding my own. The scripture here is saying that I am withstanding, coming against the devil. I put on the whole armor of God so that I can withstand Him victoriously.

Now, we are going to look at what the preparation of the gospel of peace is. How do I shod my feet? I know how to put on my shoes naturally in the morning, but how do I do it spiritually? How do I shod my feet with the preparation of the gospel of peace? What is the gospel of peace?

The Lord began to show me from scripture. Let's go to Romans 10 to see what it means to have your feet shod with the gospel of peace,

**Romans 10:1-3** "Brethren, my heart's desire and prayer to God for Israel is that they might be saved. For I bear them record that they have a zeal of God, but not according to knowledge. For they being ignorant of God's righteousness, and going about to establish their own righteousness, have not submitted themselves unto the righteousness of God."

In the last chapter we talked about Adam and Eve coming up with their own covering. They put on the fig leaves to be their own righteousness. But our righteousness is as filthy rags in His sight. There is nothing you can do by yourself that will ever be enough. There are not enough good deeds, charitable organizations for you to work for or for you to give to that will make up the righteousness of God. It is never enough. It will never work. Only His righteousness will ever do.

**Romans 10:4-15** "For Christ is the end of the law for righteousness to everyone that believeth. For Moses describeth the righteousness which is of the law, "That the man which doeth those things shall live by them. But the righteousness which is of faith speaketh on this wise, Say not in thine heart, "Who shall ascend into heaven (that is, to bring Christ down from above:) Or, Who shall descend into the deep? (that is, to bring up Christ again from the dead.) But what saith it? The word is nigh thee, even in thy mouth, and in thy heart: that is, the word of faith, which we preach; That if thou shalt confess with thy mouth the Lord Jesus, and shalt believe in thine heart that God hath raised him from the dead, thou shalt be saved. For with the heart man believeth unto righteousness; and with the mouth confession is made unto salvation. For the scripture saith, "Whosoever believeth on him shall not be ashamed. For there is no difference between the Jew and the Greek: for the

**same Lord over all is rich unto all that call upon him. For whosoever shall call upon the name of the Lord shall be saved. How then shall they call on him in whom they have not believed? and how shall they believe in him of whom they have not heard? and how shall they hear without a preacher? And how shall they preach, except they be sent? as it is written, How beautiful are the feet of them that preach the gospel of peace, and bring glad tidings of good things!"**

We are looking at several things. First, what is the gospel we are supposed to shod our feet with? We have to find out what it is before we can shod our feet with it.

The word gospel simply means the good news, that which is good to the hearer. What is good news to someone who is going to hell? They don't have to go there. What is good news to somebody who is sick? They don't have to be sick anymore. What is good news to somebody who is bound by the devil? They can be delivered. What is good news to somebody who is facing a financial crisis? There is a way out. This is good news and this is what Jesus came to share with people. You don't have to go through the bondages of satan, you don't have to be bound. You can be set free. That was the good news of Jesus Christ. We are to shod our feet with the good news.

Shod means we are to attach the good news to our feet. Attach to our feet means to attach to our foundation. The foundation of our spiritual walk with God is supposed to be the good news of Jesus Christ. That is what I stand on. I am standing upon the solid rock, Christ Jesus. Jesus Christ is the gospel. He is the good news. I am attaching to my feet the good news of Jesus Christ, my foundation. This is what it means to shod your feet with the gospel.

**Acts 4:11-12; "This is the stone which was set at nought of you builders, which is become the head of the corner.**

**Neither is there salvation in any other: for there is none other name under heaven given among men, whereby we must be saved."**

There are people in the world who do not believe that Jesus is our way of salvation. Jehovah Witnesses do not believe that Jesus is the way of salvation. The Mormons do not believe that Jesus is the way of salvation. The Jews do not believe that Jesus is the way of salvation.

So what makes our foundation strong and what enables us to stand upon a solid rock is that Jesus Christ is our means of salvation. There is no other name given among men under heaven whereby we can be saved except through the precious wonderful name of Jesus. There is no other way, no other door. In John 10, He said He is the door. If you try to come in by any other way, you are a thief and a robber. The only way in is through Jesus. He is the only way to heaven. Nicodemus, in John 3, wanted to know how to get to heaven. Jesus said you must be born again. You must be born of water and the blood in the natural. You must also be born of the spirit in order to enter into the kingdom of God.

How are we born again? Through the precious blood of Jesus by the Spirit of God we are born into the family of God. This is the foundation that enables us to stand strong. If you don't have this foundation, there is a weak place in your armor. Satan will get through it. If you don't have your foundation, every other part of the armor is shaky.

The very thing you stand on are your feet. They are the foundation. Everything else is sinking sand. Upon Christ the solid rock I stand. I stand upon Jesus as my means of salvation, as my way of salvation. He is the way, the truth and the life. No man can come to the Father but by Jesus. He is the only way.

What does it mean for us to be shod with the preparation of the Gospel of peace? It means that we have stability in God.

**Colossians 2:7; "Rooted and built up in him, and stablished in the faith, as ye have been taught, abounding therein with thanksgiving."**

We are rooted and grounded in Jesus Christ. He is the corner stone of our building. Without Him nothing will stand. The building will fall without Jesus Christ as our foundation.

**1 Corinthians 3:11; "For other foundation can no man lay than that is laid, which is Jesus Christ."**

Jesus came to give us full salvation. That is our foundation. It is what we stand upon. He is salvation and there is no other way to be saved.

**2 Timothy 2:19 "Nevertheless the foundation of God standeth sure, having this seal, The Lord knoweth them that are his. And, Let every one that nameth the name of Christ depart from iniquity."**

Those who know the Lord are His, belong to Him. This is part of the foundation also. You get to know the Lord through salvation. You have a relationship with Him in this salvation and you are standing on Him. There can be a nice foundation, but if you don't stand on it you will have no salvation. You have to find the foundation and stand on it.

You have to get to know the Lord in the power of His resurrection, what He is like in this salvation and partake of this salvation for yourself. You have to have an experience of this salvation based upon the Word of God. Don't try to have an experience and then try to find it in the Bible. It has to be based upon the Word of God.

There are many who try to find one scripture in the Bible that will agree with their experience. That is dangerous. You don't want that. We want to stand upon the Word of God, upon Jesus Christ as the solid foundation upon which we can stand. When the storms of life come against us we won't fall. We will not be destroyed for we are founded upon the Rock. He is the Rock.

Jesus called Peter petra, little stone. Peter had just made the confession that Jesus was the Christ, the son of the Living God. When Jesus answered that upon this rock, He was not talking about Peter. Peter was not a stable rock. He was a person, a man. Jesus was talking about the rock of confession of faith that Peter had in Jesus Christ when he said to Jesus, "Thou are the Christ the son of the Living God." That was the solid foundation. That is the foundation that is sure. That is the foundation we can stand on. Jesus said that upon this rock He would build His church and the gates of hell would not prevail against it. The rock is that Jesus Christ is the son of the living God, that He is the means of salvation. He is the only way that you and I can be born again and enter the kingdom of God. That is our foundation. That is what makes us stable. That is what we need.

## Be Prepared

**Ephesians 6:15; "And your feet shod with the preparation of the gospel of peace;"**

Be prepared. Provide and make yourself ready with the knowledge, with the experience, and with the life of God in you so that not only are you standing on that foundation, but also are able to share that solid foundation with others. And you are prepared to do it. You are ready to give an answer to every man with the faith that lies within you. You are ready to share with others why Jesus is so special to you. Ready to answer why you can smile in the midst of the storm. Ready to share why you love to go to church all the time. You can share with people about the salvation of Jesus, what it means to be saved, what it means to be on that solid foundation of Jesus Christ the only way, the only truth and the only light. There is not another realm. There is not another way.

Satan preaches a message that says as long as you worship somebody, you will be all right. That is a lie. You will go to hell worshipping something else. You will burn in eternal flames if Jesus is not your savior. There is no other way, no other name under heaven given unto men whereby you can be saved except through the precious, holy name of Jesus. Jesus said He is the door. There is no other way in so, it is not all right to worship something else. It is not all right if they worship God, but don't accept Jesus. It is not all right if you go to church, but don't accept Jesus as your Lord. It is not all right if you do all the right types of things, but don't make Jesus your Lord. It is not by works of righteousness that I have done. I can't do anything that will make me righteous in myself. It is the gift of righteousness that is given to us by faith when we accept Jesus Christ as our Lord and Savior. Those things are given to us. We must make ourselves ready to share that good news with others.

When someone has a need, when someone wants to know about Jesus we are quick to share it. 2 Timothy 4:2 tells us to preach the Word in season and out of season. Be ready at all times. I Peter 3:15 says to be ready always to give an answer to every man that asks you a reason for the hope that is in you with meekness and fear. Be ready to give an answer. Be ready to share why you believe what you believe.

## Sozo

Now let's look at what being saved really means. The Greek word for saved is sozo.

In Mark 5:23 Jairus had a daughter who was dying.

**Mark 5:23; "And besought him greatly, saying, My little daughter lieth at the point of death: I pray thee, come and lay thy hands on her, that she may be healed; and she shall live."**

The word healed in this passage is sozo, which means to save. If we could have been there, we would have heard Jairus say, "I pray thee come and lay your hands upon her that she may be saved and she shall live." The word healed can be translated saved or healed depending on what the problem is.

We are talking about what salvation is. This is the gospel of salvation through Jesus.

**Acts 14:9; "The same heard Paul speak: who steadfastly beholding him, and perceiving that he had faith to be healed [sozo].**

The man had faith to be saved, to be sozo.

**Luke 8:36; "They also which saw it told them by what means he that was possessed of the devils was healed [sozo]."**

Someone who is delivered from demons is saved from satan's power. Someone who is healed of sickness is saved from sickness. Someone who gets a financial miracle is saved from a financial disaster. Someone on their way to hell receives Jesus and is saved from hell.

Salvation is an all-inclusive term. Jesus came to give us all of the benefits of salvation.

**Matthew 8:25; "And his disciples came to him, and awoke him, saying, Lord, save [sozo] us: we perish."**

Jesus came to save you from disaster. He came to heal you just like He came to set you free from satan's power. He came to meet your financial needs just like He came to save you from hell. It is all the same thing.

**Romans 10:9 "That if thou shalt confess with thy mouth the Lord Jesus, and shalt believe in thine heart that God hath raised him from the dead, thou shalt be save [sozo]"**

In the Strong's Concordance, sozo is safety, healing, preservation, protection, to be saved from sin, to be saved from destruction. It has everything in there all under the word sozo. Jesus came to give you the whole thing. He came to give you full salvation.

He didn't just want to save you from your sin to keep you out of hell. He also wants to heal your body when you get sick, to meet your needs when you have a need, to deliver you from the attacks of satan. Because God made you spirit, soul and body He is concerned about your spirit, soul and body. He wants to give you full salvation. This is the foundation of the gospel, that we have received full salvation. Shod your feet with it, share it, tell everybody Jesus has saved you.

How do you receive the full salvation?

Confess that Jesus is Lord of all that He did come up out of the grave. God raised Him up by the power of the Holy Ghost. He is Lord of all. He is Lord over your finances. If you belong to Him, if you asked Him to be your Lord then He is going to be the Lord of your body just like He is the Lord of your spirit. He is going to be the Lord of your pocketbook. He is going to be the Lord of your family. He is going to be the Lord of everything that touches your life. Jesus is Lord of all.

This is the foundation that we must shod our feet with. We must attach it to our feet and stand firmly. Jesus is Lord of all, and He has given us full salvation.

That is shodding your feet with the gospel of peace. The gospel will bring peace. It brings peace to your heart. When the storm comes, He is Lord of all.

What about the word of reconciliation? What if we went forth with the word of reconciliation saying, "God has not imputed sin to you. He has already provided a way of salvation. He is not holding a thing against you. He just wants you to come on in. He is not putting a guilt trip on you or pulling you down." The world already knows it is going to hell so why do I need to walk up and tell them that to their face. I should be telling them the way out. That is all they want to hear anyway.

"How can I be free so that I don't have to go to a place called hell? How can I be healed so that I won't be sick, lose my job and lose my finances? How can I have my needs met? Does God care about that? Does God care about my children? Does God care that they get enough to eat?"

When you start sharing the gospel of peace with people, you will change lives. Jesus came to give full salvation. He came to give you the whole thing. He wants to heal your body and save you from hell. He wants to make you a new creature in Christ Jesus so that you won't go to the place that wasn't prepared for you anyway. It was prepared for the devil and his angels. You will be a trespasser if you go there.

I have heard people ask why God allows people to go to hell. He doesn't want them to go there. He made a place they could go to called heaven. But you will go with whomever you serve as god. You will go to his home. If you serve the devil and want to serve him then one day you will go to be with him forever. If you serve God and love God, one day you will go to be with Him in His home forever.

I choose to serve Jesus Christ, to stand on a firm foundation and to accept what Jesus has given to me as His child. Are you a child of God? Stand on a firm foundation. It is just as easy for you to be forgiven of sins as it is for you to be healed in your body. It is just as easy for you to get a financial miracle as it is for Jesus to forgive you if you ask Him to. We have made it difficult. We think it is hard. "It is easy for Him to forgive my sins, but hard for Him to heal my body." No! In fact, most of the time it all happens at the same time. James 5:15 talks about forgiving someone their sins and healing their body at the same time. It is all provided. Everything is taken care of. We serve a mighty God and He is not against us. He loves us and is for us.

God is not even against the sinner. He loves the sinner and hates the sin. God wants to save the sinner. He has already provided for their salvation and is waiting for them to receive it. If you are sick, God has already provided for your healing. He is waiting for you to receive it. If you have a financial need and need God to move in your life, He already has a miracle for you if you have been planting and giving. He is just waiting for you to receive it. If you are bound up in any way in your life, under depression, under the load that satan has brought against you, God already has provision for you to set you free.

# THE SHIELD OF FAITH

**Ephesians 6:10-13; "Finally, my brethren, be strong in the Lord, and in the power of his might** [our strength is not in ourselves but in the Lord]. **Put on the whole armor of God, that ye may be able to stand against the wiles of the devil.** [Why?] **For we wrestle not against flesh and blood, but against principalities, against powers, against the rulers of the darkness of this world, against spiritual wickedness in high places. Wherefore take unto you the whole armor of God, that ye may be able to withstand in the evil day, and having done all, to stand."**

There is a time to stand when you have done everything. You keep standing and keep on believing that the Lord is going to bring it to pass. That is the testing time. If you pass the test, you get the operator's license. That is the time you learn to stand, regardless of the situation, until it breaks. It will break as long as you don't break. Hold steady because in due season you will reap if you faint not.

We haven't learned to stand in faith. If God's Word is true then this thing has to break sooner or later. The only thing we are looking at is not God failing, but us failing God. If we will keep on standing, we will see the manifestation. Sooner or later it will be forth coming. I have seen that in my Christian walk. It is to keep persevering and holding on by faith. When you have done all, keep on standing until the manifestation comes. It is forth coming. You will not have to stand like that forever. It will break for you as long as you don't break before it happens, as long as you don't begin to waver in your faith, as long as you don't give up.

**Galatians 6:9, "Let us not be weary in well doing: for in due season we shall reap, if we faint not.**

The Bible tells us in Galatians 6:9 that in due season we will reap if we faint not. We have to know how to stand and how to continue to stand. The standing process is the hardest thing we will ever do. One thing that will help you is your confidence in God. If you have true confidence in God, you will be like Abraham strong in faith and giving glory to God. You will not waver because of the situation. You will not waver because of circumstances even if it takes years. You will keep on standing and God will bring it to pass for you.

**Ephesians 6:14-16; "Stand therefore, having your loins girt about with truth, and having on the breastplate of righteousness; And your feet shod with the preparation of the gospel of peace; Above all, taking the shield of faith, wherewith ye shall be able to quench all the fiery darts of the wicked."**

Shield (Greek: thureos, thoo-reh-os') means going through something. It is actually talking about a gate or a door of faith. Doors and gates have a two-fold application. They can be used as protection to keep anybody from trying to come in. They can also be used to go out and be able to do things. They enable you to go forth, to go through. As I began to study this I looked at John 10 and at what Jesus said He was.

## FAITH

We are going to talk about the phrases faith in, of faith, through faith and by faith.

**John 10:7; "Then said Jesus unto them again, Verily, verily, I say unto you, I am the door of the sheep."**

Who is our faith in? Jesus.

**1 John 5:4; "For whatsoever is born of God overcomes the world: and this is the victory that overcometh the world, even our faith."**

It is not faith in faith, but faith in somebody. It is confidence and knowledge that there is somebody bigger than you and I who has the ability, the strength, the resource to take care of us and meet every need we have. That is what faith is all about. It is getting to know somebody and having confidence in somebody who is bigger than we are, has ability beyond our ability, and has resources beyond our resources. Jesus had unlimited resources, unlimited ability, unlimited power to do anything we need. If we can begin to put our faith in that, put our faith in the God who is more than enough, put our faith in the God who is not limited then that is true faith.

It is not faith in faith, but faith in a person.

We know that Jesus said He is the door. Remember, door is the same Greek word as shield. He literally is our faith. He is who your faith is in and He is where your faith comes from. We know that faith comes from hearing, but hearing what? The Word of God. Who is the Word of God? John 1:4 tells us that in the beginning was the Word and the Word was God. Verse 14 says the Word dwelt among us.

**John 1:14; "And the Word was made flesh, and dwelt among us, (and we beheld his glory, the glory as of the only begotten of the Father,) full of grace and truth."**

Jesus is the Word, the reason to believe. Because of Him we have faith. We have a person to have faith in. Otherwise faith would have no solid foundation. It would mean nothing. Jesus is the personification of faith.

**John 10:8-9; "All that ever came before me are thieves and robbers: but the sheep did not hear them. I am the door. By me if any man enter in, he shall be saved, and shall go in and out, and find pasture."**

How are we saved? Through faith in Jesus. That is how we enter in. Finding pasture is finding provision.

If we were to study about the shepherd, the sheep and the sheepfold we should see that the sheepfold had a doorway, but it didn't have a door. The shepherd would lay down in the doorway and become the door. That is why Jesus said He is the door. He will be there to protect the sheep from anything that would try to come in to harm them. The sheep trust in the door. They had faith that the door would protect them. They had faith that the shepherd would protect them. He was also the way for them to go in and out and find pasture. That means provision. They could go out through the door and find plenty of green pastures. They could go out through the door to the cold waters and have a lot to drink. They could enjoy life by going in and out through the door. That is provision as well as a protection.

This is so much more than we realize about the armor of God. The armor is not just protection. It is also a way of provisions. It is a way for you to spoil the devil and get everything you need. Take it away from the devil. Take it back from the devil. Make him return it seven fold. You have caught the thief.

## Faith In

First, I want you to notice that you have to have faith in Jesus.

**Acts 3:16; "And his name through faith in his name had made this man strong, whom ye see and know: yea, the**

**faith which is by him hath given him this perfect soundness in the presence of you all."**

This scripture was about a man at the Gate Beautiful who was not able to walk. Peter and John came along and gave him what they had.

**Acts 3:6-8; "Then Peter said, Silver and gold have I none; but such as I have give I thee: In the name of Jesus Christ of Nazareth rise up and walk. And he took him by the right hand, and lifted him up: and immediately his feet and ankle bones received strength. And he leaping up stood, and walked, and entered with them into the temple, walking, and leaping, and praising God."**

The Scribes, Pharisees and those already in the temple wanted to find out what was going on and they were told it was through faith in His name. It is through faith in Jesus that the answer comes. That is our foundation for faith. Faith has to have focal point or it is not strong. It means nothing. We have to be able to focus on someone who is bigger than we are, who has more ability than we have and is able to take care of us, someone we can put our confidence and trust in. That is faith.

There is faith in. We know from Romans 4:20 that Abraham was strong in faith. Who was he believing in? He was believing in God who said so. He was believing in God who calls those things that be not as though they were. He was believing in a God who had more than enough power to take care of him and give him a child even when he was beyond the age of natural possibility. Why could he believe that? Because of a person. Our faith has to be tied to a person.

## By Faith and Of Faith

It is not only faith in but also by faith.

**Galatians 2:20; "I am crucified with Christ: nevertheless I live; yet not I, but Christ liveth in me: and the life which I now live in the flesh I live by the faith of the Son of God, who loved me, and gave himself for me."**

Jesus even gives us His faith and His ability to believe. He comes along and does a wonderful work in us.

After we look at by faith, we are going to look at of faith. Romans 12:3 says God has dealt to every man a measure of faith.

So, Jesus had given to us His ability to believe. What usually happens is that we don't use what He has given us. We don't plant the seed with our tongue. We don't speak it out. In Mark 11:23 Jesus was talking about faith the size of a grain of mustard seed. He was saying that the words we speak are our faith seed. Plant the seed. Get it out there. It will produce if you will just believe and speak it. Take that little seed of faith and put it in the form of words. Speak it out and it will perform. Get your seed out there. It is not enough to have seed in a nice little bag all wrapped up because it will never produce. You have to get your seed out of the bag and planted in the ground.

It is so amazing that from the very beginning of Genesis, God said that as long as the earth remains there will be seedtime and harvest. In everything, natural and spiritual, there is seedtime and harvest. With your faith, there must be seedtime and harvest. There must first be seedtime, then harvest time. Use the faith that God has already placed in you. He has already dealt you out a measure of it. Take it and speak it out.

**Mark 11:23; "For verily I say unto you, That whosoever shall say unto this mountain, Be thou removed, and be thou cast in the sea; and shall not doubt in his heart, but shall believe that those things which he saith shall come to pass; he shall have whatsovever he saith."**

It is believing and speaking. The speaking is planting the seed. The believing enables the seed to produce. You have to have it. That is the seed of faith.

## Through Faith

**Philippians 3:9; "And be found in him, not having mine own righteousness, which is of the law, but that which is through the faith of Christ, the righteousness which is of God by faith:"**

**Hebrews 11:3; "Through faith we understand that the worlds were framed by the word of God, so that things which are seen were not made of things which do appear."**

Through faith we get the understanding. Through faith we receive the provision.

Through Jesus I have the understanding. Through Jesus I have my provision. Through Jesus I have my needs met. Through Jesus my prayers are answered.

In all of these things we can say it is faith in Jesus, faith by Jesus, the faith of Jesus and faith through Jesus. All of the shield is Jesus. Jesus is your shepherd, your protector at the same time He is your provision. He is both your provision and your petition. He is there to do in your life what needs to be done if you can vocalize in your spirit who you are believing in. Then begin to study about what He is able to do. Look and see if there is anything He cannot do. Are there any limitations to Him? If He can do anything and there are no limitations in Him then I have to say that I can truly put my faith in Him, put my confidence in Him as the door of protection and provision.

**Psalms 37:40; "And the LORD shall help them, and deliver them: he shall deliver them from the wicked, and save them, because they trust in him."**

They trust in Him, in the door, in the shield, in Jesus, in a person. It is not just trusting in faith as faith, but is faith in a person who is more than enough, faith in a person who has no limitations, faith in the Son of God. Faith in an omniscient, omnipresent God, in a God who spoke all of the world into existence. We know from John that the Word was the one who spoke everything into existence. He made everything that was made.[6] He is the power. He is the glory. He is the anointing. He is everything I need. He is my shield. He is my way of protection. He is my way of provision. He is the shield for me. David said that the Lord was a shield for him, the glory and the lifter of his head.[7] David knew who his shield was.

Who is the shield of faith? Jesus. Who is your provision? Jesus. Who is your protection? Jesus. And He is the shield.

I found out that the shield was not a little thing. It was big enough to cover, the size of a door. Many times the armor bearers would lift them up, move them ahead and stick them in the ground. They would stand behind and hold them while the soldiers were doing the warfare throwing the spears, fighting in the combat. It was a protection. It was also provision when it came time to spoil the enemy.

Our Lord is concerned about us. He doesn't just want to keep us safe from the devil. He wants to meet every need we have.

**Psalms 23:1-3; "The LORD is my shepherd; I shall not want. He maketh me to lie down in green pastures: he leadeth me beside the still waters. He restoreth my soul: he leadeth me in the paths of righteousness for his name's sake."**

Look at the shepherd. Look at what all He does for you. Not just a protection, but also provision. Remember the shepherd is the door. He got down in the doorway and became the door for the sheep. Our trust, our confidence, our faith is Jesus. He is the door.

We should have faith in Him. We should have the faith of Him, have the faith by Him and through Him we have faith. He is our faith. He is our reason for living. He is our reason for existing. He is our reason for eternal life for He is eternal life. From the beginning to everlasting He has always been. He will always be. We can reach out and grab hold of that shield, grab hold of the hem of His garment hang on and know that He will provide for us. He will be there for us.

All things are possible to him who believes Jesus said in Mark 9.

## Testimony

I want to share a testimony with you.

Several years ago the Lord spoke to us to go and work with another pastor. We had visited him, sensed in our spirit that he had the same vision we did and that God wanted us to work with him. There was no promise of a salary, of a house or anything else. We just knew that God wanted us to go.

Like Abraham we packed up and took off for the country that God called us to. When we got there we didn't know we wouldn't have a house to live in and we didn't have the money to get one. We began to trust the Lord, put our reliance in Him. We started to work with the pastor and said, "Lord, whatever you order you pay for. Whatever you want done you have the power and the ability to make sure the finances and resources are there."

We began to trust the Lord and very slowly things began to open up. God took care of a mobile home for us and it didn't cost us anything to live there. We began to work 40 to 70 hours a week with no promise of any money. We had three children, payments and bills that needed to be taken care of. There were a lot of times I sensed I should hunt up a job, but I knew what God said so I worked in the Lord's work. I believe that if you don't work, you don't eat. I was working for the Lord and putting in my time. The Lord had spoken to me and said that He would pay me for the hours better than any man could. I got excited and decided that I was going to put in some hours. God began to move. People in the church would walk up to me and hand me $100. They would hand me a check for $200. There were a lot of weeks when $400-500 was handed to me. God began to move and to do a work.

There were weeks when it was tough. I remember one week when the rent, utilities, car payment and insurance were all due. Things were weighing heavy on me. The kids needed shoes and we needed groceries. Connie spoke a word to me that I believe was from the Lord. She told me to grab the kid's hands and shout, holler, dance, jump and praise the Lord for meeting our needs. I did not feel like doing that. I felt low, like a snake crawling on its belly. It was hard. My flesh did not want to do that at all. I don't even think my mind wanted to do it. My spirit needed lifting up.

We got in there and grabbed hands, jumped, hollered, shouted. "Praise God, every need is met. The Lord is supplying the money. It is coming in today in the name of Jesus. Praise God, satan is bound. The needs are being met. Praise God." We began to praise the Lord every need was met even though we didn't have any money. Faith is believing it before you see. You have to believe it is done before you see it and then it will manifest itself.

**Mark 11:24; "Therefore I say unto you, What soever ye desire, when ye pray, believe that ye receive them, and ye shall have them."**

It is after you believe that you receive what you believed will manifest.

The more we praised the better I felt. I got happy in the Lord. When we first started praising it took everything I had in me. I felt like such a hypocrite. I felt terrible, but the more I worshipped the Lord, the more I shouted, hollered, jumped and praised God that the need was met, the better I felt. I know we must have kicked the devil that day.

That very day people started bringing over groceries. We hadn't told anybody. In a couple of days the finances started coming in. Different things begin to happen. I saw God bring checks in the mail. Nobody owed me any money. They were love offerings and God was the one who supplied them.

We need to see Him and see that praise really does work. It is not just a religion, it is reality. These are principles that work if we will work them. If we don't work them, they won't work. It is like our cars. They won't work by themselves. We have to get in and operate them. We have an operator's license because we studied the manual to find out how to operate them. We passed the test. We know how to turn the thing on, steer it, put in gas and get down the road safely. God wants us to do the same thing with the Word of God in our spiritual walk, in our spiritual life. We need to learn the manual so we can pass the test and get our operator's license. We have to know how to operate our faith, know how to walk in faith, know how to live by faith, know how to speak our faith and know how to receive by faith.

# HELMET OF SALVATION

**Ephesians 6:17; "And take the helmet of salvation, and the sword of the Spirit, which is the word of God:"**

What is the helmet of salvation? How do I put it on? It is not the same as picking up a regular helmet and sticking it on my head. When I put a helmet on my natural head it won't cover my spiritual head. It won't protect me from satan. Since we don't wrestle against flesh and blood we can't put the armor on in a fleshly way. The armor has to be put on it a supernatural, spiritual way.

Helmet means a covering of protection for your head. I found in my studies that it is the covering for your soul: mind, will and emotions.

**James 1:21; "Wherefore lay apart all filthiness and superfluity of naughtiness, and receive with meekness the engrafted word, which is able to save your souls."**

Souls in the Greek is psuche (psoo-khay'). This is where we get our word psychology. It is the word for our mind, our ability to think. We know the engrafted word has the ability to save our minds, to save our thoughts, to save us from coming under attack in our mind. If satan can destroy or dominate your thought life, he has dominated you. If he can keep you from thinking about God and keep your mind off of the Lord then he has dominated you. That is why in Isaiah we read that God will keep in perfect peace those whose minds are stayed on Him.[8]

**I Thessalonians 5:23; "And the very God of peace sanctify you wholly; and I pray God your whole spirit and soul and body be preserved blameless unto the coming of our Lord Jesus Christ."**

We know that we are a spirit being who possess a soul and live in a body.

**Hebrews 4:12; "For the word of God is quick, and powerful, and sharper than any two-edged sword, piercing even to the dividing asunder of soul and spirit, and of the joints and marrow, and is a discerner of the thoughts and intents of the heart."**

Save, in James 1:21, is sozo and it means to protect, to bring health to your mind. The Word of God is there to protect your mind, to bring health to your mind. There is much talk today about mental health, about people having their minds destroyed. The reason is because they do not have their minds stayed on God. They have their minds on the world, on their problems, on themselves. Because of the lust of the flesh, the lust of this world, the lust of the eyes and the pride of life their minds are totally destroyed by satan. He has come in and brought guilt, condemnation and destroyed the minds of men.

We see from the Word of God that Jesus has given us a covering, a helmet. That helmet is the Word of God. He has given us the helmet to cover our minds and to cover our thoughts, to enable us to have mental health and to enable us to have protection against satan. Satan's inroad into your life is through your mind. We need to put on the spiritual helmet of salvation.

The root word for salvation is also sozo. It means the knowledge of salvation, the knowledge of healing, the knowledge of prosperity, the knowledge that you don't have to go to hell but to a place called heaven, the knowledge that He came to give you life and that more abundantly, the knowledge of all that He has provided for you. If you can gain that knowledge and implement it in your life then it will become a helmet of salvation against satan's thoughts and against satan's arrows that fly into your mind to destroy you.

We put on the helmet of salvation in three ways. We know that the helmet is the knowledge of the Word of God. It is knowing what Jesus has provide for you. It is knowing what He has given to you.

Acquiring the knowledge in the following ways will bring about the helmet of salvation. You will literally be putting it on. You are taking it to yourself. You are literally putting it on in the spirit.

## Gain the Knowledge

First, if we know that the Word of God is the helmet then we have to gain the knowledge of full salvation and what Jesus has provided for us. We are full gospel people so we believe in the full gospel. We believe the gospel is not only salvation from eternal punishment, but also peace of mind and healing for our bodies. We believe God wants to meet our needs. We believe that by His stripes we are healed. We believe that He is there. We believe the Word of God and what it has to say about full salvation. We believe in the full gospel. When we gain the knowledge of that, it will protect us and provide for us.

**1 Timothy 4:13; "Till I come, give attendance to reading, to exhortation, to doctrine."**

Reading the Word of God is not only reading it by ourselves. In the context of this verse, it also means the public reading. That means we need to be at church to hear the reading of the Word. We need to hear it by exhortation which means preaching and doctrine which is teaching of the Word.

We need the reading of the Word, good preaching and good teaching in order to gain the knowledge of what we can have in Jesus Christ. But be careful of who you listen to. Faith comes by hearing, but so do doubt and unbelief. If someone comes along and starts putting down divine healing to you, don't listen to them. That won't gain you the knowledge you need to put on the helmet of salvation. If someone comes along and starts putting down the fact that God meets our needs, don't listen to them. You don't need to hear that. It won't help you put on the helmet of salvation. If someone starts putting down the baptism of the Holy Ghost with the evidence of speaking in other tongues, don't listen to them because they will not help you put on the helmet of salvation. You need to gain the knowledge of it, not someone putting it down which won't help you or lift you up.

We need to gain the knowledge through reading the Word of God ourselves, through the preaching of the Word and through the teaching of the Word. Paul asked a group of people if they had received the Holy Ghost since they had first believed. They said they didn't ever know there was such a thing as the Holy Ghost.[9] How else could they receive if they didn't know? You cannot receive anything without the knowledge of it first. You receive Jesus as your Lord and Savior because you received the knowledge of it. Many people are healed because they receive the knowledge of it. People are delivered because they receive the knowledge that is given forth. The Word of God is preached and then it is confirmed. The Word of God is shared and then the confirmation comes. So we gain the knowledge of it.

God gives us anointed teachers and preachers of the Word who can bring forth the Word of God and bring forth anointed teaching that can help you get the knowledge you need. It is more than just the preaching because preaching is exhorting you. I can exhort you all day. You ought to be healed. Come on and let's get healed. That will never get you healed. Oh, you ought to get out there and win the lost. You sit there and say that you know you ought to. Then the teacher comes along and gives you the how to. You need the inspiration that the preacher gives and the how-to that the teacher gives.

Then, you read the Word yourself as another means of gaining the knowledge so that you know what they are preaching and teaching is the truth. We are gaining the knowledge so that we can know what they are preaching and teaching is the truth. Be careful of what you read, careful of what you see and be careful of what you hear because eventually it will get into your heart. We are looking at gaining the knowledge of the Word.

## Expand the Knowledge

Once you gain the knowledge, you need to expand the knowledge. That is the second part.

**2 Timothy 2:15; "Study to show thyself approved unto God, a workman that needeth not to be ashamed, rightly dividing the word of truth."**

As a child of God it is your responsibility to study. The preacher begins to preach and teach, gets your interest going and you go home to study what is being preached or taught.

This scripture tells me that if you are not studying, you won't know the truth. You won't rightly divide it. You will take anything somebody says and say it is the truth because you heard it. Your preacher said it so it must be the truth. That doesn't necessarily make it the truth. That is why we are to study. We are to take what is being preached, what is being taught and begin to study it ourselves. We are to see if what we are being taught is really the truth.

In John 5:39 Jesus told the Scribes and Pharisees to search the scriptures. They thought they had eternal life, but the scriptures testified of Him. He was saying that if they studied the scriptures like they should, they would find Him in every book in the Old Testament. All they had to do was study it. The people were taking what the Scribes and Pharisees were saying and believing them instead of studying for themselves. Later on we find out in the book of Acts that there were some who began to study it for themselves to see if these things were really true.

**Acts 17:10-11; "And the brethren immediately sent away Paul and Silas by night unto Berea: who coming thither went into the synagogue of the Jews. These were more noble than those in Thessalonica, in that they received the word with all readiness of mind, and searched the scriptures daily, whether those things were so."**

Study is a noble thing to do. They did daily Bible study, not just Bible reading. Reading is the start to study, but not the end or the in-between. It is not the body only, but the introduction to the information. Reading is the introduction to the body of information that you need. Don't just stop with the introduction, you will never get the meat. You have to study to dig out the meat and to dig out the complete truth.

**John 8:31-32; ".....If ye continue in my word, then are ye my disciples indeed; And ye shall know the truth, and the truth shall make you free."**

We need to get into the Word and let the Word get into us.

## Dwell on the Knowledge

Once you have gained the knowledge and once you have expanded the knowledge you move on to dwelling and meditating on that knowledge. This is the third step. You begin to dwell on the things of God that you have been studying. You begin to think on these things.

The Lord began to speak to me about Philippians 4:8-9. What are those things that talk about praise and good things? That passage in Philippians simply shares with us that we are to think about the Word. There is nothing more lovely than God's Word. There is nothing more pure.

Psalms 19 talks about God's Word being pure, like gold, precious. When Paul was talking about thinking on the good things the people of Berea knew what he was referring to because they knew the book of Psalms. They knew he was saying to think on the Word of God and what it had to say about that which is lovely, that which is pure, that which is precious and that which will bring praise into your life.

We begin to dwell upon those things that we have learned and that we have been gaining knowledge of. Mary, Luke says, pondered those things she had heard and learned in her heart. She kept them precious. To ponder something means to go over and over it in your mind and in your heart. It means to put your thoughts upon those things until they continue to roll over and over inside of you. That is dwelling on the knowledge.

**1 Timothy 4:15; "Meditate upon these things; give thyself wholly to them; that thy profiting may appear to all."**

What happens when I begin to meditate on those things that I have learned and have expanded the knowledge of them? I begin to profit by them. That ties in perfectly with Psalms 1.

**Psalms 1:1-3; "Blessed is the man that walketh not in the counsel of the ungodly, nor standeth in the way of sinners, nor sitteth in the seat of the scornful. But his delight is in the law of the LORD; and in his law doth he meditate day and night. And he shall be like a tree planted by the rivers of water, that bringeth forth his fruit in his season; his leaf also shall not wither; and whatsoever he doeth shall prosper."**

The word meditate simply means to give your full attention to, to think upon, to ponder, to muse, to chew, to digest. That is exactly what this scripture is talking about. It is chewing, digesting and talking to yourself about what the Word of God is saying through meditation. Meditation is the digestive process for your spiritual body. It enables you to digest the Word and give strength to your spiritual body just like natural digestion gives strength to your physical body.

When you eat something in the natural, your body begins to break it down into smaller parts and then begins to slowly assimilate it into your system. The process begins immediately when you start eating it. That is exactly what happens to us when we go through these three steps of gaining the knowledge, expanding the knowledge and meditation and then dwelling on that word. Our spiritual body begins to break it down slowly. That is why we need to take time in meditation and think on the Word of God. Take time to think about what Jesus has provided for you, how you can live the Word, how you can do the Word, how you can walk in the Word and how to assimilate that knowledge into your life. Then your spiritual man begins to draw the nutrients out so you can begin to do something with that.

**Joshua 1:8; "This book of the law shall not depart out of thy mouth; but thou shalt meditate therein day and night, that thou mayest observe to do according to all that is written therein: for then thou shalt make thy way prosperous, and then thou shalt have good success."**

You make your way prosperous by meditating on the things of God, the Word and the truth of the Word. You make your way successful by meditating on the things of God and what God has given you. We begin to gain this knowledge and begin to meditate upon the expanded knowledge that we have received. We need these in order for us to walk in them.

**2 Corinthians 10:4; "(For the weapons of our warfare are not carnal, but mighty through God to the pulling down of strong holds;)"**

We have been talking about armor. We have said that it is not only a defensive weapon, but an offensive weapon also. It not only protects you, it also reaches out there and grabs the provision we need from God. It defeats the devil. When you gain the knowledge of the truth, satan is defeated in your life. When you gain the knowledge that you can be born again and you are no longer in satan's kingdom, satan is defeated in your life. When you gain the knowledge that you can be healed instead of being sick, satan is defeated in your life. When you gain the knowledge that you can walk in God's provision, satan is defeated in your life. When you gain the knowledge that you can claim your household for Jesus Christ, satan is defeated. God has given us household salvation. When you realize that, have studied it, expanded the knowledge, meditated on it and received it by faith, satan is defeated.

The helmet of salvation is not only protective, but also offensive. It defeats the devil in your life.

# Strongholds

**2 Corinthians 10:5; "Casting down imaginations, and every high thing that exalteth itself against the knowledge of God, and bringing into captivity every thought to the obedience of Christ;"**

Now let's look at how satan brings strongholds into your life.

It starts with a thought. Satan will bring a thought against you. Then he will expand that thought. The thought is the knowledge. The same way we overcome the devil is the same way the devil overcomes us. Think about it. First of all he brings the thought, which is the knowledge of something evil or destructive.

Then he brings the full knowledge of that and expands that knowledge, backing it up carefully. "Look at what happened over here. Remember what happened to that person last year. You remember way back when. Look at this. Look over here." He expands the knowledge.

Then the next step he brings is the imagination because you start meditating on those things. The more you meditate the more you can see yourself being affected in that way.

Now satan has a stronghold there. You are battling a stronghold.

Let's reverse it. Instead of talking about satan doing that, let's look at what will happen if we do the same type of thing. We will get a stronghold over the devil. First comes the thought "Hey, I can be healed. The Word says I can be healed." Now that is a thought, isn't it? Then I begin to gain more knowledge, read the scriptures and study, hear preaching and teaching on it. That gets me all excited. I even begin to enter into some study on it. Then I start meditating on it. That is the next part - the imagination. I start meditating on it and before long I start seeing myself walking in health. I can see it in my mind. I can see myself healthy and well. Already I have a stronghold over the devil. I am about to be healed.

Let's reverse it again to see how satan comes to bring temptation into our life. A worldly man is tempted to get involved in theft. Here comes the thought, "You don't have any money. You ought to go steal something." Then satan begins to show him how he can do it. "Look here. This guy has a farm with machinery and sometime he doesn't take the keys out of it. You could go over there and steal it." Here comes all this knowledge. Satan keeps adding knowledge because the person is listening. Before long the person begins to study and plan out how he could do it. Then he starts seeing himself doing it. The next step is he is doing it.

Reverse it once more. Here is a child of God who needs to have his needs met. He doesn't know his rights in Jesus. He opens his Bible and reads the verse that says, "My God shall supply all your needs."[10] That is a thought, God meeting all his needs. He picks up a book on prosperity and begins to read it. Then he turns on the television and there is some preacher teaching on it. He goes down to the full gospel church and the preacher starts talking about having your needs met through Jesus. He opens his Bible and starts studying it. Imagination comes along and he starts seeing himself prosperous and God meeting his needs. The next step is that he starts receiving from God. Maybe a job opportunity opens up. Maybe he gets a raise on the job he already has. Maybe someone comes by who owed him some money and they pay him. Maybe an insurance company paid a claim that they wouldn't before. There are several thousands of dollars on the guy's table now because of this process.

These things happen. We are looking at how to put on that helmet against temptation. When you put it on, you also begin to receive things from God.

**2 Peter 1:3; "According as his divine power hath given unto us all things that pertain unto life and godliness, through the knowledge of him that hath called us to glory and virtue:"**

Through the knowledge of God we receive all the things that pertain to life and godliness. We are looking at the natural things and the spiritual things being supplied.

Through the knowledge of Him who called you to glory and virtue is how you put on the helmet of salvation. It not only protects you from the devil and what he tries to bring against you by way of thoughts, but it also will bring the provision of God. I have noticed that is true with all the parts of the armor. I see protection and provision through every part of the armor. It is exciting. I see it as protecting and as a weapon.

You and I don't have to be defeated or waver in our minds. You can set your mind on the Lord and on the things of God. Begin to study. Begin to read. Remember the Bereans. They did it daily.

Take what I have been showing you. Get an exhaustive concordance of the Bible and begin to do word studies. My Bible is number one and my concordance number two. That is how I study all the time, along with that I have other books. I will spread them out on the floor and get down there so I can get to all my books. I have books everywhere, all over my desk. I start running references, doing word studies and get out my dictionaries. I want to know the truth. The truth will set us free.

# SWORD OF THE SPIRIT

**Ephesians 6:17; "And take the helmet of salvation, and the sword of the Spirit, which is the word of God:"**

We are going to learn exactly what the sword of the Spirit is. And we are going to learn how to effectively use it.

Just opening your Bible and reading a scripture is not the sword of the Spirit. One translation I read said, "the sword with the Spirit, use it" when it was talking about the sword of the Spirit.

If you have a Vine's Expository Dictionary of New Testament Words, you can study and begin to understand what logos and rhema mean. Only by understanding those things can you understand what the sword of the Spirit really is. In one place it says, "the injunction is to take the sword of the spirit which is the Word of God." Here the reference is not to the whole Bible as such, but to the individual scripture which the Spirit brings to our remembrance for use in time of need. The only prerequisite is that we would store that information in our minds and in our hearts. Then the Holy Spirit begins to touch in our lives the scriptures that we have stored and they will be a flaming sword against satan.

I want to show you that Jesus is the logos. I am going to show you that the logos became rhema and how it happened. Again, using Vine's, the word logos means simply the fact of the Word of God. In the Bible there are facts. It is a fact that Jesus in the Christ, the Son of the living God. He is the logos, the fact of God.

**John 1:1; "In the beginning was the Word, and the Word was with God, and the Word was God."**

Word in this passage is logos.

**John 1:14; "And the Word was made flesh, and dwelt among us..."**

The logos was made flesh.
Later we see that He became the rhema word, the rhema of God. He did not remain the logos, the fact of God, but became the truth of God.
As we get into this you will see what you need to do to speak the rhema because the rhema is the sword. The rhema is what will cause things to happen. I am going to show you through the Word of God how to have a Word from God, how to receive a rhema from God. You have to first do the message in the chapter on "The Helmet of Salvation" before you can go on to receiving a rhema from God. You have to gain the knowledge, expand that knowledge and then the dwell on that knowledge. The Holy Spirit begins to choose parts of that knowledge that will become a flaming sword, a two-edged sword against satan. Notice the sword has two edges on it. Two-edged means two mouths. It is a spoken Word against the devil and a spoken Word for what I have need of. It cuts the devil to pieces and also delivers unto me what I need. It is much like you taking a sword, cutting the stalk of bananas off a tree and delivering provision to yourself.
The two-edged sword cuts against the devil. It also releases provision into your life. It has two mouths. That means you have to speak against the devil, rebuke satan and speak for your provision.

**Luke 3:21-22; "Now when all the people were baptized, it came to pass, that Jesus also being baptized, and praying, the heaven was opened, And the Holy Ghost descended in a bodily shape like a dove upon him, and**

**a voice came from heaven, which said, Thou art my beloved Son; in thee I am well pleased."**

Jesus was baptized by John the Baptist and also by the Holy Ghost.

**Luke 4:14; "And Jesus returned in the power of the Spirit into Galilee: and there went out a fame of him through all the region round about."**

**Luke 4:22; "And all bare him witness, and wondered at the gracious words which proceeded out of his mouth. And they said, Is not this Joseph's son?"**

They wondered at the gracious words that came out of His mouth. They couldn't believe that He was who they thought He was because of all of the words. What happened to Him before that? He was baptized of the Holy Ghost, filled with the Holy Ghost and was led by the Holy Ghost. And He returned in the power of the Holy Ghost. The Holy Ghost is the factor that makes rhema out of logos.

Jesus was the logos. He was the written fact of God, but He did no miracles until after He was baptized of the Holy Ghost. Then rhemas came out of His mouth.

When you are full of the Word and full of the Spirit, the Spirit of God will begin to test you and tell you to speak something out. You will speak that scripture out and see the creative power of it right before your eyes as the Holy Spirit begins to quicken the scripture, begins to make it alive inside of you. He gives you the very verse you need that will release the anointing of God through those Words. You will see the miracle power of God right before your eyes. When you open the Bible, pluck out a scripture and start speaking it, you will see nothing happen.

It is true that angels and demons will hear your words. Angels are activated by your words. When you are full of the Spirit, you are led by the Spirit even in what you say. When you are flowing in the power of the Spirit, God will give you a message. When you speak it out, it will change lives because the Holy Ghost gives you the message. You shouldn't just open the Bible, take one scripture out and say "This would be a good one." You wait upon God until the rhema of God comes forth by the Spirit of God. Then when you go forth and preach that message, the anointing of God is upon it. God anoints those words, quickens those words, empowers those words by His Spirit until people say, "Never a man spoke like this man."

**Luke 4:32; "And they were astonished at his doctrine** [at His teaching for He was a teacher]**:for His word was with power."**

That means His Word had the power of the Holy Ghost in it. That is the rhema of God.

The Word of God is a seed that has not yet been germinated. It is the logos. The Holy Ghost is the water. You apply water to a seed that is in the soil, germination takes place and you have life. John 7:37-39 talks about water being likened to the power of the Holy Spirit.

**John 7:38-39; "He that believeth on me, as the scripture hath said, out of his belly shall flow rivers of living water. (But this spake he of the Spirit, which they that believe on him should receive: for the Holy Ghost was not yet given; because that Jesus was not yet glorified.)"**

The Holy Spirit is likened unto living water. The Word of God is likened unto a seed. Our heart is likened unto soil. If you plant a seed in dry soil it has no life. You only have a seed sitting there in dry soil. When the moisture begins to come from the Spirit of God, it begins to germinate that seed and begins to release the power that is in that seed to produce what that seed is.

We now want to give you some ways to receive rhemas from God, which are the Sword of the Spirit. First though, you must fill your mind with the Word of God. We find them in I Timothy 4:13-16.

**1 Timothy 4:13-16; "Till I come, give attendance to reading, to exhortation, to doctrine. Neglect not the gift that is in thee, which was given thee by prophecy, with the laying on of the hands of the presbytery. Meditate upon these things; give thyself wholly to them; that thy profiting may appear to all. Take heed unto thyself, and unto the doctrine; continue in them: for in doing this thou shalt both save thyself, and them that hear thee."**

There are five things we can do to receive rhemas from God. Those things are the reading of the Word, the study of the Word, meditating on the Word and also prayer.

The first thing the scripture says to do is read the Word of God. We need to be people who spend time every day reading the Word of God, but also studying the God's Word.

Secondly, we need to study the Word of God. We need to research the Word through word studies and looking up corresponding scriptures and meanings. Let's read what 2 Timothy 2:15 says.

**2 Timothy 2:15; "Study to show thyself approved unto God, a workman that needeth not to be ashamed, rightly dividing the word of truth."**

Thirdly, we are also to listen to good preaching and teaching of the Word. The preaching of the Word is the proclaiming of the truth of the Gospel of Jesus Christ. The teaching is the explanation of the Gospel. The proclaiming and explaining of the Word is very necessary in beginning to receive rhemas from the Lord.

**Matthew 4:23; "And Jesus went about all Galilee, teaching in their synagogues, and preaching the gospel of the kingdom, and healing all manner of sickness and all manner of disease among the people."**

We need to listen to good teaching and preaching. Luke 5:15-17 speaks about Jesus teaching the Word of God, the people coming to hear and to be healed of Him. They came to hear the teaching and preaching of the Word in order to be healed.

The fourth thing we need to do is to meditate on these things that our profiting may appear to all.

**Psalms 1:1-3; "Blessed is the man that walketh not in the counsel of the ungodly, nor standeth in the way of sinners, nor sitteth in the seat of the scornful. But his delight is in the law of the LORD; and in his law doth he meditate day and night. And he shall be like a tree planted by the rivers of water, that bringeth forth his fruit in his season; his leaf also shall not wither; and whatsoever he doeth shall prosper."**

Those four things are the reading of the Word, the studying of the Word, the listening to preaching and teaching, the meditation of God's Word, but there is also prayer. Prayer is the fifth thing.

In Luke 8 Jesus is teaching about the parable of the sower. He is talking about the Word of God being in people's hearts. Verse 6 says it did not bring forth any fruit because it lacked moisture. So we see that we need moisture with the seed. We need the Holy Spirit to come. The Holy Spirit comes in many ways, though mainly when we begin to pray and seek the face of God.

In John 7:37 we read a verse where Jesus is speaking.

**John 7:37-39; " In the last day, that great day of the feast, Jesus stood and cried, saying, If any man thirst, let him come unto me, and drink. He that believeth on me, as the scripture hath said, out of his belly shall flow rivers of living water. (But this spake he of the Spirit, which they that believe on him should receive: for the Holy Ghost was not yet given; because that Jesus was not yet glorified.)"**

Jesus was saying that when He went back to the Father, He would release the Holy Spirit. If we would believe on Him, He would release living water.

Now let's look at how the Holy Spirit came on Jesus in the first place. In Luke 3 we have the story of Jesus being baptized by John the Baptist.

**Luke 3:21-22; "Now when all the people were baptized, it came to pass, that Jesus also being baptized, and praying, the heaven was opened, And the Holy Ghost descended in a bodily shape like a dove upon him, and a voice came from heaven, which said, Thou art my beloved Son; in thee I am well pleased."**

In our scriptures we see that the Word needs the moisture of the Holy Spirit in order for it to germinate and produce. We also see that Jesus spoke of this water being the Holy Spirit that would come. Those who believed on Him would receive the special anointing of the Holy Spirit, which would be water to water the seed.

Jesus was praying at the time He was baptized. The Holy Spirit came upon Him as He was praying. I believe that as we press into God, spend time in prayer the Holy Spirit will come upon us. If we have adequately fed the Word into our heart though reading, studying, listening to teaching and preaching and meditating on the Word of God in prayer, then God will cause the seed of the Word to come up and come alive within us. We will receive rhemas from God. The rhemas of God are the sword of the Spirit when the seed of God's Word is planted in the soil of the hearts of men.

Today, spend time in the Word and in prayer and receive your sword of the spirit. That is the two edged sword that will stop the enemy and bring provision in your life.

# CONCLUSION

**Ephesians 6:10-13; "In conclusion, be strong in the Lord - empowered through your union with Him; draw your strength from Him - that strength which His [boundless] might provides. Put on God's whole armor - the armor of a heavy- armed soldier, which God supplies - that you may be successful to stand against [all] the strategies *and* deceits of the devil. For we are not wrestling with flesh and blood - contending only with physical opponents - but against the despotisms, against the powers, against [the master spirits who are] the world rulers of this present darkness, against the spirit forces of wickedness in the heavenly(supernatural sphere). Therefore put on God's complete armor, that you may be able to resist *and* stand your ground on the evil day[of danger], and having done all [the crisis demands], to stand [firmly in your place]." Amplified Bible**

P aul comes to the end of his letter to the Ephesians and summarizes his letter by saying, "In conclusion...be strong in the Lord and put on the whole armor that you may be successful when you stand against the devils tactics."

**John 10:10; "The thief cometh not, but for to steal, and to kill, and to destroy: I am come that they might have life, and that they might have it more abundantly."**

Satan wants to make us miserable when God wants to make our lives blessed. That's why Paul says in verse 13 to put on God's complete armor so that we can resist and stand firm in our place of total success and blessing.

We have learned that the armor is not only defensive, but also offensive. It is not only for our protection, but also for our provision. We have also learned that God's armor is His Word revealed and applied to every area of our lives.

When we put on the armor we are putting into action the revelation of God's Holy Word and applying it to every vital part of our lives where satan would try to steal from us. In doing this we are stopping the enemy and bringing about the full manifestation of the goodness of God's best in our lives. In other words...we are **arming ourselves for victorious living.**

[1] Colossians 2:15
[2] Philippians 4:19
[3] James 1:17
[4] 1 John 5
[5] 2 Corinthians 5:17
[6] John 1:3
[7] Psalm 3:3
[8] Isaiah 26:3
[9] Acts 19:2
[10] Philippians 4:19

www.ingramcontent.com/pod-product-compliance
Lightning Source LLC
LaVergne TN
LVHW041714060526
838201LV00043B/723